FEET

HUMAN BODY

Robert James

The Rourke Press, Inc.
Vero Beach, Florida 32964

PHOTO CREDITS
All photos © Kyle Carter except cover and page 18 © Frank
Balthis; pages 7, 12, 17 © Jerry Hennen

Library of Congress Cataloging-in-Publication Data

James, Robert, 1942-
    Feet / by Robert James.
        p. cm. — (Human body)
    Includes index.
    Summary: Describes the anatomy of the human foot and
includes information on foot problems, foot care, and the feet of
some animals.
    ISBN 1-57103-106-5
    1. Foot—Anatomy—Juvenile literature.   [1. Foot.]
I. Title II. Series: James, Robert, 1942- Human body
QM549.J36 1995
611'.98—dc20   95–19285
                                                        CIP
                                                        AC

Printed in the USA

TABLE OF CONTENTS

FEET

A man handed a shovel to his son. "You've got two good feet," the man said. "One is for standing on, and the other is for pushing the shovel into the ground."

Two good feet and a shovel can dig holes, but a boy's or girl's feet will do much more.

Feet are designed most of all to support our weight when we stand. They help make it possible for us to stand without falling over.

USING YOUR FEET

Feet help us to stand still. They also help us to move from place to place while standing upright. With our feet to stand on, we can walk, jog, run, kick, and climb.

By wearing skates, skiis, flippers, or roller blades, we make our feet even more useful for certain purposes.

Cross country skiis make foot travel through the snow fast and fun

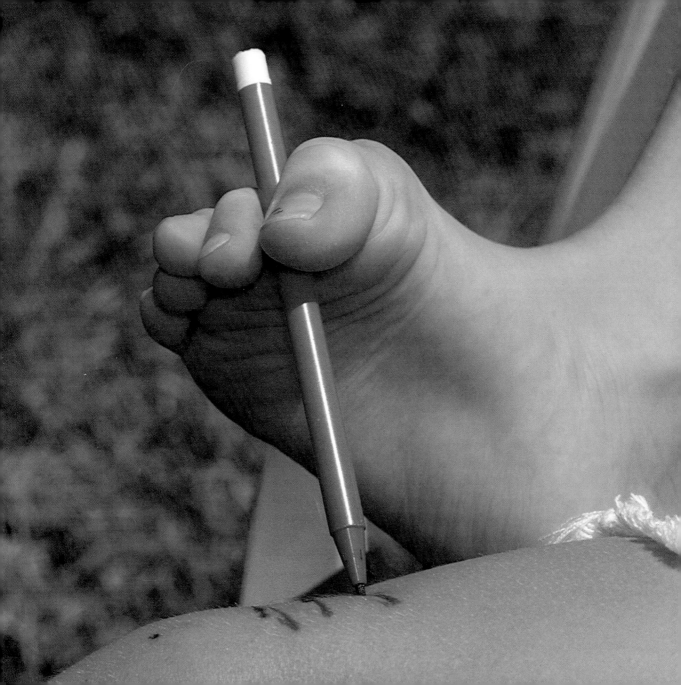

HANDS AND FEET

In some ways, our hands and feet are similar. The hands have five fingers, and the feet have five fingerlike toes.

Feet are stronger and heavier than hands. After all, they have a load to carry. Still, like hands, feet assist with our sense of touch. The toes, like fingers, can grasp and even pick up some things. Many people who have lost the use of their hands can use their toes skillfully to draw and write.

In a pinch, toes will grasp a pen

THE OUTER FOOT

The underside of a foot is called the **sole** (SOLE). The sole is padded with fat, especially at the rear of the sole, known as the heel.

Feet take a steady pounding from carrying weight. The fat pad between the foot bones and skin cushions the impact of walking and running.

The raised arch of the foot rests in the center of the sole. People with low arches are "flat-footed."

Feet are built to take the pressure of steady walking

Dancers step lightly on their feet in rhythm with music

Soccer brings a flurry of flying feet

INSIDE THE FOOT

Inside the foot is a **maze** (MAYZ) of bones, blood vessels, **nerves** (NERVZ), fat, muscles, and **ligaments** (LIHG uh ments).

A human foot has 26 bones. Fourteen of them, called **phalanges** (FAL an jez), are in the toes.

Ligaments are strong bands of flesh. They help keep foot bones in place and move the foot at the brain's command.

A model of a human foot bares its bones

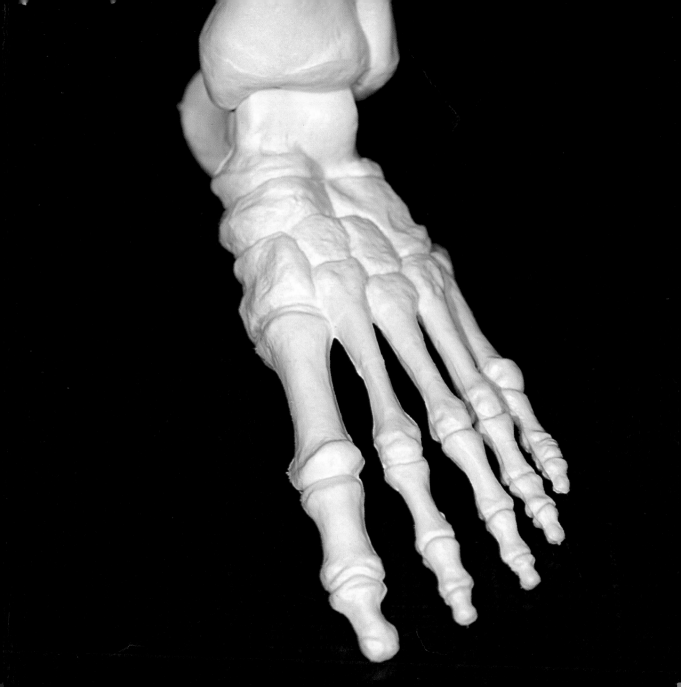

FEET AND BRAIN

The sense of touch in your feet is linked to your brain. Nerves in the skin of your body are little "feelers." Nerves are sensitive to touch and temperature. Nerves send signals to the brain.

The brain receives the signals. We feel those signals as a touch or as heat or cold.

The brain also sends messages to your feet, causing them to step, or kick, or do what you want them to.

Oozing mud and cool water are a treat to hot, tired feet

FOOT PROBLEMS

Being a foot isn't easy. Feet take the heavy impact of walking or running, and sometimes they suffer because of it.

Toes, like fingers, can be frostbitten if they become too cold. Toes can also be bothered by the cracking skin and itching of athlete's foot. Athlete's foot is a common skin disease caused by a **fungus** (FUNG gus) that loves dark, damp places, like the space between toes!

FOOT CARE

Foot doctors are **podiatrists** (po DI ah trists). They work with both common foot problems and more serious ones.

A foot doctor can prescribe shoes or medicine that will help a patient. A doctor can operate on the foot if a serious problem arises.

You can often avoid a foot problem by taking proper care of your feet. Wear shoes that fit well. Rest tired feet, and don't let your feet become too hot, too cold, or too moist.

A physical therapist fits a runner to special soles that will aid his aching feet

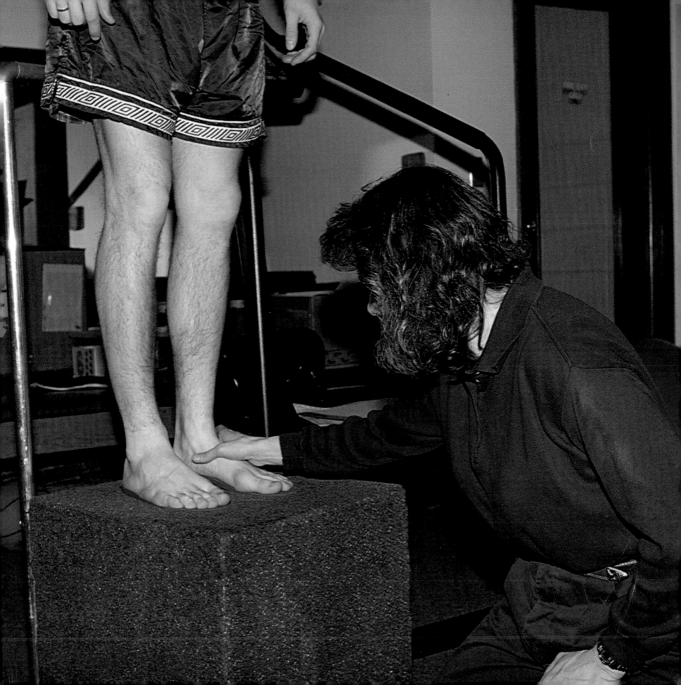

ANIMAL FEET

Few animals walk upright on two feet. Those that do—kangaroos, for example—have larger, stronger hind feet than front feet.

Most animals, though, walk on four feet. Those animals usually have front and hind feet that are much alike.

Some of the most humanlike feet belong to monkeys. Monkeys, like humans, have fingerlike toes. Monkey toes do a better job of grasping than human toes. That is because their feet are designed for living in the tree tops.

Glossary

fungus (FUNG gus) — a large group of living, plantlike things, one of which causes athlete's foot

ligament (LIHG uh ment) — a tough band of flesh that helps keep bones in place

maze (MAYZ) — a complicated arrangement of parts

nerves (NERVZ) — the sensitive "feelers" in flesh that send messages to the brain

phalanges (FAL an jez) — any one of the toe or finger bones

podiatrist (po DI ah trist) — a foot doctor

sole (SOLE) — the underside of the foot

INDEX